The Crisis
and
Analysis of John Stuart Mill's Life

The Crisis
and
Analysis of John Stuart Mill's Life

Kathleen Thomas, B.A.

The Pentland Press Limited
Edinburgh • Cambridge • Durham

© Kathleen Thomas 1994

First published in 1994 by
The Pentland Press Ltd.
1 Hutton Close
South Church
Bishop Auckland
Durham

All rights reserved.
Unauthorised duplication
contravenes existing laws.

ISBN 1 85821 110 7

Typeset by CBS, Felixstowe, Suffolk
Printed and bound by Antony Rowe Ltd., Chippenham

INTRODUCTION

John Stuart Mill has left a lasting impression on future generations through the unusual manner in which he was educated, and the brilliant scholar that he developed into.

But he also possessed qualities that made him stand apart from the other famous men in history. He had a profound interest in the execution of social duties and how they affected the public. He devoted a lot of time to publishing articles and doing active service to improve the lot of the less fortunate. For that tendency to improve conditions for the betterment of mankind, he was seen by some as wavering and one who lacked determination. Although he was not conceited, he was well aware of his abilities, and could afford to ignore malicious remarks.

His entire education was carried out in his father's home, and he spent all his childhood years in the company of his father's peers. That accounted for his serious demeanour as a young man.[1]

His qualifications spanned many disciplines, philosopher, economist, administrator among others. His scientific books and essays are still as highly valued in intellectual circles in this era as they were when he first wrote them.

Other works include: *Dissertations and Discussions*, periodicals, essays, reprints, *Subjection of Women*, *On Liberty*, *Auguste Comte*, his *Autobiography* and many others. Mill was

---

[1] L. Stephen, *The English Utilitarians* (London, 1900) Vol.II, p.315.

still a child when the duty of teaching his younger brothers and sisters fell on his shoulders. He had no time to indulge in any form of sports or play. When not studying his own lessons, he had to mark their papers and organize the lessons for the next session. As he was so much further advanced educationally than the younger children, he could find no common ground between them. He was a solitary child who had to depend entirely on his own resources.

Mill did not find his father approachable enough to discuss problems with him. Had he done so, he most probably would have been told to find a solution on his own, as that was the method that James Mill applied in training him. Seen from that angle, it would appear that his father had been unnecessarily harsh and cruel in his treatment of him. Yet, had he gone through the usual channels of education, there would not have been a "John Stuart Mill", who has passed on so much to posterity.

Kathleen Thomas, B.A.

THE CRISIS

For years John Stuart Mill wandered in a dreamy world in which he visualized himself as the leading character of a new world order. He was convinced that his ultimate happiness and contentment would be achieved by the pursuit of this utopia. The extensive classical education instilled in him by his father at the tender age of three years, made him confident of his ability to fill a post of such varied demands. Concurrently, he would be able to utilize talents that would otherwise lie dormant.

When he realized that his hopes and aspirations were not well grounded, in fact highly unlikely, he became depressed and entered a prolonged emotional crisis. Former activities no longer had any appeal, the sense of loss (of his dream) creating a profound emptiness in his life. He began to analyse his motives, his background training and the magnitude of the project. Only then could he gain a perspective on his problem and begin his slow recovery.

Selections from Bentham's *Westminster Review* sparked off the controversy in his mind. He identified in this writer's work all the conscious and unconscious thoughts that he had been formulating in his mind over the passage of time. He was convinced that here was the meat of his life's work. His sympathies echoed those who laboured on the reform of matters of national importance. In his opinion, no greater tribute could be rendered to one's country than the elimination of negative conditions.

Mill was convinced of his intellectual superiority and had no doubt that he would excel in his role as "World Leader". His new-found ideas took precedence over all other concerns, dominating his mind to an unhealthy degree. He was on fire. He strove to find new avenues of study and research that would glorify his position as a future world leader.

Mill was further convinced that his quest was of dire importance at the advent of activity. He identified himself with this movement during the years that he harboured his obsession. In this period, he neglected his writing and speaking engagements and kept his professional activities to the minimum. The internal transformation, of which he was hardly aware, began to influence his character and psyche. This was, in part, due to his exploration of new fields of study, but more so by the stimulation of new ideas that anticipation had inspired. These internal changes were signposts that would eventually disperse the apprehension that had robbed him of his peace of mind. He had, however, not as yet reached that stage of revelation.

The rejection of the foundation of his life's building blocks, i.e. his education and the influence of his father, made the crisis deeper. Life lost all meaning. He had lost the will to live as he could no longer find any reason or purpose to justify his existence. Misery became his constant companion. Coleridge's "Dejection" illustrates his plight thus:

> "A grief without a pang, void, dark and drear, A drowsy, stifled, unimpassioned grief, which finds no natural outlet or relief in word, or sigh, or tear,"[1]

Somewhere in the recesses of Mill's mind he was convinced that his particular training had fitted him for a unique career, but he had allowed his ideas to expand beyond practical or possible reach. He never doubted his destiny (or the delusions of grandeur) that he would attain his desired goal. However, perhaps as consequence of the depression and his altered thought processes, he concluded that what he had in mind was not feasible without being rejected by an outside agency.

---

[1] John Jacob Coss (Preface), *Autobiography of John Stuart Mill*, published from the original MSS., Columbia University Library (Columbia University Press, New York, 1944), p.94

His rigid training had made him self-reliant. When he encountered problems he solved them by his own efforts. By nature very detached, he had difficulty forming intimate relationships, and lived a somewhat alienated existence, unable to confide in or trust his friends. He told himself that he needed freedom to pursue his interests, but became acutely aware of his emotional poverty when the crisis came. He felt as if he was stranded on an isolated island, with no hope of returning to civilisation. He could not turn to his father, the one closest to him, in this condition. No mention was made of his brothers and sister. He appeared to be a man very much on his own.

His crisis, in part self-inflicted, was devastating. He felt that all avenues were closed to him, and deliberately created and nurtured the fantasy that absorbed so much of his time and thought. He searched his mind for consolation among the books of his library, but found nothing to justify the obsession that enveloped him. A doctrine, instilled in him by his father, aided him slightly:

> "the object of education should be to form strongest possible associations of the salutary class; associations of pleasure with all things beneficial to the great whole, and of pain with all things hurtful to it."[2]

In a broad sense, this doctrine covered some of Mill's thoughts. "Associations of pleasure with all things beneficial to the great whole" described his attitude and frame of mind in which he found so much satisfaction. Although he wanted to be of service to mankind, we see him engaged in a great deal of thinking, and very little action towards his goal. He seemed to derive a lot of satisfaction in "struggling" along with the others. He experienced the pain of disappointment, reverse conditions and delay.

Mill ruminated endlessly through the various schools of philosophy, searching and occasionally finding some link to the ideas that clouded his mind.

---

[2] Ibid., p.96.

He found new ideas to develop and assist him but they did not identify closely enough with his desired aim. "Benthamism", another version of the Utilitarian doctrine, was undoubtedly the one that was partially responsible for his miasmic state. Suggestions from other philosophical schools were an added factor. He was an active member of debating societies, and published numerous articles. He collected data and chance remarks with the subliminal hope that they would be useful to him in the fulfilment of his ambitions. A debating society, after all, was the most likely arena for finding answers to his problem, as all matters of importance in the literary world were sifted through these chambers.

He began a rigorous self-examination of his character and what motivated his actions, discovering qualities of which he was not previously aware. Most importantly, he realized that his actions could have stood the benefit of analysis or reflection before being put into practice. From that point on, new ideas grew and, through analysis, he was able to see the light where before, all was darkness.

He could not believe that he had not tried this before, and could perhaps have been spared the tortures of delusion. He found analysis to be a powerful tool to disseminate and weaken prejudice, and was able to separate his ideas which had previously become entangled and distorted.

He realized that even the most profound knowledge could easily become warped if left intellectually unexamined.

Mill blamed his education for his suffering. Because his training had been so intense, he had become precocious, arriving at conclusions prematurely. Since self-reliance had always been stressed upon him as a prime value, it was natural that he should form his own opinions and act upon them independently. Had his delusion become realized, he would never have known the value of self-analysis, and the importance of community. He had to change. Eliminating false ideas, and patterns of behaviour of long duration, would present a formidable task, if he were to transform himself and reveal his authentic nature.

Part of the problem was the achievement of too much, too early. He had, in literary matters, distinguished himself from other boys of his years. He took this as natural, finding himself more at par with his father's contemporaries. He was aware, and also gratified, that his father encouraged this atmosphere as he wanted him to be advanced in all subjects. He believed his ideas to be invincible and would have considered an alteration in his behaviour or character as unnecessary, if not impossible. Now, in the depths of misery, his thought habits were already undergoing transformation.

He began to analyze and apply reason before making definite statements, managing to maintain a normal outward appearance in spite of the internal upheaval. He went through the motions of composing and delivering speeches, many of which he confessed to remembering next to nothing. As he said:

> "I have been so drilled in a certain sort of mental exercise, that I could still carry it on when all the spirit had gone out of it."[3]

For a long time, things remained unchanged. Of all the arts, music was his favourite, but he found he could no longer enjoy it as before. He was extremely pessimistic in general and did not have much hope in his future. He recapitulated all the time and energy his father had endowed him with and regretted how disappointed he would be in him. Fundamentally, although they agreed on certain subjects, such as politics, etc., as individuals they were not alike, and Mill despaired of the enormous emotional chasm between them. This was "the unkindest cut of all."

Having resigned himself to what he believed to be his unfortunate destiny, Mill was relieved to learn through reading Marmontlel's *Memoires*[4] that his dark feelings were normal and that he could hope again for a good life. He recognized that the veil of darkness which he had passed through had been a period of self-discovery and revelation of his true nature.

He saw that happiness was not determined by changing the

---
[3] Ibid., p.98
[4] Ibid., p.99

exterior conditions of one's life, rather it depended on the peace and joy one finds within, and by good works or self-sacrifice to a worthy cause. His nature and his understanding of knowledge deepened.

The change taking place in Mill's life was a gradual process. Whereas before he placed the blame on his education, he now knew that it was his interpretation that had been at fault. He saw that intellect and culture in themselves could never pose a threat to society or the individual, but that the mode of application could be erroneous and thus create misunderstanding. He was grateful for his well-developed mind, now that he could channel his thoughts in the right direction. He recaptured his joy in music, but with a critical sense that was not there before. He listened now with analytic scrutiny, anxious to understand elements that he had not recognized in the past.

Continuing his introspection, Mill became aware that the flaw which he observed in himself was not wholly personal but rather a characteristic of the human condition, which is destined to experience dejection and frustration as part of life. He searched for solutions among poets, philosophers and realists. He could find no answer in Byron's poems, they were too reminiscent of his present frame of mind. Wordsworth, on the other hand, soothed him with his images of green fields and the beauties of nature.

The rural settings of Wordsworth's poetry relaxed his mind. He knew there were greater poets but they did not express joy and beauty to the reader as Wordsworth did:

> "What made Wordsworth's poems a medicine for my state of mind, was that they expressed, not mere outward beauty, but states of feeling, and thought coloured by feeling, under the excitement of beauty."[5]

Mill used the works of Wordsworth to declare his first return to his former habits. A debating society was formed between his

---
[5] Ibid., p.104

friend Roebuck and himself to fight out their differences in opinion in relation to Wordsworth and Byron. Roebuck held that Byron's poems were a valid representation of human life. Later, they were joined by others with similar ideas and the stimulation of these meetings helped to release Mill from his worrisome thoughts. Many in the debating group became aware of the changes in Mill, and he re-evaluated his relationships, becoming much more critical, maintaining only those who possessed the qualities he desired in friendship. Roebuck was one of those who did not share some of his ideals, causing them to eventually drift apart. Mill withdrew from the Debating Society and carried on his studies in private.

At this time, he had no desire to reveal his inner thoughts to the public, as he was experiencing many changes within and new ideas were flowing through his mind that he was anxious to record. He was conscious of this process, fusing new ideas with the old, thus avoiding a complete intellectual schism. He realized that he had adopted many of his father's and Bentham's theories. He researched and questioned issues that he had previously accepted at face value.

He now analyzed the motive as well as the action in any given theory before accepting it. He began to criticize his father's attitude without bias, agreeing with him in principle, but felt that something was fundamentally wrong with his philosophical conception of the theory. He felt that both Macaulay and his father had erroneous ideas in their approach when dealing with the subject.

Using the critical approach, Mill examined his thoughts and was able to identify the false ideas that he harboured. He realized that his overly logical approach, particularly in relation to his theories, was extremely biased and ego-centred.

He realized his errors in judgement and dedicated his work in the future to truthful examination of his concepts and no longer indulged in fanciful daydreams as he had done in the past.

His new insights into logic and the sciences inspired him to publish an article on ". . . Logic of the Moral Sciences . . .".[6] In this

---

[6] Ibid., p.113

article he expressed his new ideas and his political stance. In retrospect, Mill found that his new discoveries were already universally well-accepted, although he himself had previously not held these views. In his words:

"... but the rediscovery was to me a discovery, giving me plenary possession of the truths, not as traditional platitudes, but fresh from their source...".[7]

Later, when suffering through a period of depression, he found a measure of comfort in his enlightened thoughts and his new philosophy. The doctrine of "philosophical necessity" (in his terms) became so much a part of his self-imposed responsibility, that it weighed him down. He gradually saw that the word "necessity", as applied to human actions, carried a misleading association. He realized that one's environment directly contributed to the formation of character, coupled with individual desire and life experience.

From that point on, his bouts of depression were much less frequent than in the past. He also became aware that many famous authors of varying nationalities held similar views.

He was particularly attracted to writers of the St. Simonian school in France,[8] whose new political thought was gaining attention. For the first time, Mill considered the natural order of human progress and the history of organic life.

He found and later illustrated the works of Auguste Comte among the St. Simonian publications. This work was very interesting to Mill as it contained the natural succession of "three stages in every department of human knowledge."[9] These discoveries helped him to gain a clear conception of the social conditions peculiar to any period. He began to view the future with new-found optimism. He hoped that the political system of these times would embrace a

---

[7] Ibid., p.118
[8] Ibid., p.114
[9] Ibid., p.116

policy based on philosophical concepts, particularly as it affected the systems of education, religion and a broad spectrum of official policies.

Another idea adopted by Mill was that of "Fatalism". This gave him some relief in the belief that many of the big issues of his life were ultimately not within his control, releasing him from a degree of responsibility for his actions. He recorded his findings in a chapter on "Liberty and Necessity", in the concluding book of his *System of Logic*.[10]

He also benefited from the writings of Carlyle, widening the narrow boundaries that existed in his creed and guiding his thought toward more productive thinking. Carlyle taught him the theory of "anti self-consciousness". Carlyle was a confirmed "Mystic", unlike Mill, creating differences between them. Mill, however, appreciated those authors who opened his mind to the fundamental principles he sought, which helped him restore his mental balance.

In reviewing Mill's experiences, one could easily conclude that it was unique, regardless of his history of depression, through a wide variety of experiences and the process of intellectual and spiritual exploration. His search for truth and meaning in his life led him down avenues of thought that would normally remain dormant in the average man of his time. Without this process of self-discovery, Mill would not have experienced the transformation that took place within him.

This transformation enabled Mill to regain his peace of mind and to better understand his fellow-man, as well as achieving a profound understanding of his own nature. He no longer blamed external circumstances, such as his education, and the influence of his father, for his misfortunes. On the contrary, he felt a new sense of appreciation for the knowledge that his father had exposed him to.

In conclusion, Mill realized that the process of analysis was the crucial tool that, when applied, stripped the subject free of

---

[10] Ibid., p.120

misconceptions, allowing truth to emerge in a pure and natural state. Only a crisis as profound as that of Mill's could have brought him to that state of realization and freedom.

ANALYSIS OF JOHN STUART MILL'S LIFE

All the writings of John Stuart Mill have left a deep impression on his public. But above all others the *Subjection of Women* 1869 (which has since been converted into a book) was so comprehensive in its forecast of future centuries, he was seen by his contemporaries as a man of towering intellectual importance. It was said of him:

> ". . . he stands as a significant figure in the history of ideas, one who straddled the eighteenth and nineteenth centuries and anticipated the twentieth . . ."[1]

Judging from his early training in disciplines of a more profound nature, the *Subjection of Women* appeared to be completely out of character and was responsible for sparking off a wide search and re-examination of his former works, in the hope of finding some clue for what appeared to be a new dimension in his literary career. It was only when his long years of intellectual friendship with Harriet Taylor Mill began to reveal the labour that both had dedicated to the writing of that book, that the significance of her importance to his personal and intellectual life become clear. The very nature of their friendship, which was fraught with difficulties from the start, would have inspired the ideas expressed in the book.

Both John and Harriet were in their twenties when they first met. Harriet was already married with two children. Both were intellectual and enjoyed each other's company. It could be seen as a meeting of the minds that broadened and developed into a

---

[1] John Stuart Mill & Harriet Taylor Mill, *Essays on Sex Equality*, edited by Alice S. Rossi (The University of Chicago Press, London, 1970) p.5

spiritual as well as an intellectual intimacy with the years.

John Stuart Mill was born in London on the 20th May 1806. He was the eldest son of James Mill, author of *The History of British India*, and the son of a tradesman who was brought to the notice of Sir John Stuart of Fettercain, one of the Barons of the Exchequer in Scotland. James Mill was sent to the University of Edinburgh through a fund established by Lady Jane Stuart (wife of Sir John Stuart), and other ladies for educating young men for the Church. He was licensed to teach when he left the University. However, he decided against that profession when he arrived at the conclusion that he could not believe in the doctrines of that Church or any other. He taught privately for a few years, then went on to work for the India House in a permanent position. John reviewed the magnitude of his father's responsibilities during those years when he had to survive on a small income. He had a large family, yet he was never in debt or any other financial difficulties.[2]

James Mill held strong political and religious opinions, and was not afraid to state his convictions freely in his writings. He did nothing by half measures, whether literary or otherwise. *The History of British India* took ten years to write, which was considered a short time in comparison to other historians who did only writing. Most of the responsibilities of the household fell on his shoulders as his wife (excellent in many ways) was of no help to him intellectually. It is not surprising that he saw life from a materialistic point of view, and looked at his son John in the light of an experiment which he could mould to his own specifications.

He was known to remark in an entry of his on education in the *Encyclopaedia Britannica* that:

> "... all mankind is born alike, with little or no significant variation in genetic potential for learning..."[3]

---

[2] *Autobiography of John Stuart Mill*, with Preface by John Jacob Cross (Columbia University Press, New York, 1944), p.2
[3] Ibid., John & Harriet Mill, pp.11-12

James Mill and Jeremy Bentham subjected John Stuart to a rigid set of rules that obliterated other natural impulses, such as emotion and the desire to mix and play with other children. John had no friends until he was a grown man, and with all his brilliant intellectuality, he lacked the normal social conventions of society. He felt himself to be the odd man out at parties, and was far more at ease with the learned group of men that his father gathered around him, with most of whom he was almost on a par intellectually. In later years, John described himself as a "dry, hard logical machine,"[4] and that was exactly how his contemporaries saw him.

His intensive education need not have impoverished his emotional life, and would not have done so had his home life been a normal one. The Victorian era, in which he lived, segregated women in a very marked way, especially in some classes where they were not considered equals to their husbands. That was the case in John's home. His mother was very much in the background, and seldom mentioned. John's highly developed mind observed the role she played, and he could not find it possible to respect her. The other children liked her, but there was no love between them.

John felt that his father's personality would have been entirely different if he had married a woman from a different background, or one who had some warmth in her. He felt that the lack of those qualities in his mother turned his father's thoughts inward. He knew the extent of his father's potentialities, even when he was passing through his emotional crisis and bitterly resented him for what he believed to be the cause of his depression, and he never lost sight of the fine qualities that he kept hidden behind a mask. When all the darkness had passed away and he was restored to health, he realized the enormous debt that he owed his father. It was one that he could never repay enough in giving him such an extensive and varied education and he could say:

---

[4] Ibid., John & Harriet Mill, p.12

"Mine was not an education of cram. My father never permitted anything which I learnt to degenerate into a mere exercise of memory. He strove to make the understanding not only go along with every step of the teaching, but, if possible, precede it. Anything which could be found out by thinking I never was told, until I had exhausted my efforts to find it out for myself."[5]

The accomplishments of John Stuart Mill covered a wide field. He was considered to be the most influential philosopher in the English-speaking world in the nineteenth century, and held profound Liberal views on man and society. He endeavoured to construct a philosophical point of view that would assist in scientific experiments which would eventually bring about individual freedom. Although he did not quite succeed in attaining what he had planned, he advanced specific ideas on morals and politics.

F. Y. Edgeworth's article on John Mill, in Palgrave's *Dictionary of Political Economy*, tell us that he wrote a brilliant article in defence of the East India Company (where he worked for thirty-six years), for the parliamentary debate on renewal of the Company's charter. When the renewal was granted, Mill retired and refused the offer as an official for Indian Affairs. Whenever his services were requested, his knowledge enabled him to meet those demands successfully.

Most of his young years were spent completely controlled by his father, and to a great extent, by Jeremy Bentham. Both visualized him as the future leader of the Utilitarian Group. At the age of fifteen, he read Bentham's literature on religious revelation and was convinced that he had found his aim in life. He imagined being a reformer of the world, with his father and Bentham to guide him, and was fired by inspiration. He worked even longer hours conducting a discussion group, editing Bentham's manuscripts and writing endless letters to the press on critical

---

[5] *Encyclopaedia of Philosophy*. Paul Edwards, editor in chief (Collier, Macmillan, London, 1967), Vol.5, p.314

matters of law. But deep within himself, he saw this outburst of enthusiasm as a phase through which he was passing, and realized that it had no meaning for him. He re-considered all the doctrines that he had imbibed and could find none to suit his particular mood. He felt that he had been drained of all emotion and weakened by the rigorous training he had passed through. But he still remained active, seeking for new avenues to give him fresh ideas. He read his favourite authors more intently, and endeavoured to make friends with some of the people whom he met. All his efforts just served as a salve to take his mind off his troubles for a brief spell. Finally, the cure was eventually started by his own ingenuity. He began to change his philosophical views, and drifted away from extreme radical opinions.

He had a conviction that he and other intellectuals should strive to find a method that would assist in world affairs and, especially in England, to emerge from the existing critical situation that she was passing through. Mill had an obsession to perform some act of major importance, and had fantasies of creating projects beyond the possibility of one person.[6] Therefore, a group of well-informed men would be the alternative to get a project started.

A lot of ideas began to circle in his mind then, amongst them the fact that reformers must adapt to the period in which they lived, particularly during critical times when people were looking for solutions and not far-fetched ideas. He believed in investigation and educating the public in the process as one went along, to fit them into changing conditions. By slow insinuation of particular issues, a general agreement could easily be arrived at.

Mill again found compatible ideas with the Comte and Saint-Simon views on philosophy of history. He found that they appreciated the value of old institutions which the Benthamites neglected to do. He also accepted their outline of history and theory dealing with social changes. He followed those thoughts for the next twenty years, but refrained from publishing a systematic account of his ideas. Instead, he wrote essays elaborating on specific

---

[6] Ibid., *Encyclopaedia of Philosophy*, p.315

issues and endeavoured to bring out the latent qualities overlooked by others in the books that he criticized. For those considerations, he was seen as "wavering and a muddled thinker" by some of his associates.[7] He did not contradict those who thought so, but only included what he considered to be sound views on philosophy in his *A System of Logic*.

In his *A System of Logic*, Mill launched an attack on "Intuitionism", and continued to do so throughout his life. He argued that Social Planning and political action should rely primarily on scientific knowledge, not on authority, custom or prescription. The first copies of *A System of Logic*, originated at Oxford, then went on to Cambridge and other universities where, at that time, most of the philosophies were worked out. The book was an instant success. With the publication of the *Logic*, Mill advanced in popularity and was able to demonstrate that "philosophy" was not confined to Theologians, but also covered a wide variety of everyday experiences.[8]

John Mill was back to normal when he made a discovery about himself. His superior education had placed him on an isolated island, and he had no one to share his thoughts with. He wrote confiding this observation to John Sterling.

> "There is now no human being (with whom I can associate on terms of equality) who acknowledges a common object with me, or with whom I can co-operate even in any practical undertaking, without the feeling that I am using a man, whose purposes are different, as an instrument for the furtherance of my own."[9]

Fortunately for him, that state of isolation did not continue for long. He was destined to meet Harriet Taylor and her husband among a group of Radical thinkers shortly after. Almost

---
[7] Ibid., *Encyclopaedia of Philosophy*, p.315
[8] Ibid., *Encyclopaedia of Philosophy*, p.316
[9] Ibid., John & Harriet Mill, p.19

immediately, Harriet and John found so much in common, it was just as though they had known each other for years. He no longer held back ideas that came rushing to his mind, and she found no difficulty in understanding them. The Unitarian Minister, William Fox, was the connecting link. He too had his own problems. He was tied to a loveless marriage and had fallen in love with Elizabeth Flower, another member of the Radical group. That helped to foster the friendship between Mill and himself. It was said that John Mill confided in him to a greater degree than to any other man with whom he corresponded. He even told him of some of his confused reactions after the crisis, when he apologized for not writing an article in the *Monthly Repository* (which Fox edited), saying:

> "If there are any rumors that I was writing anything for the "Monthly Repository" of this month, I am sorry I cannot confirm them. I have abundance of vague intentions of writing for you, but I have been very idle of late, and in fact never have been in a state more unfit for work: from various causes, the chief of which is, I think, a growing want of interest in all the subjects which I understand, a growing sense of incapacity ever to have real knowledge of, or insight into the subject in which alone I shall ever again feel a strong interest . . . I feel so unequal to any of the higher moral and aesthetic subjects."[10]

Considering that some of his most scientific works, such as *A System of Logic* and the *Principles of Political Economy*, were written after (but not immediately) that confession, he must have been at a very low ebb when he wrote to Fox. Eventually, the *Monthly Repository* came to be a valuable medium for trying out new ideas for Mill. Some were written under pseudonyms or as unsigned

---

[10] Ibid., John & Harriet Mill, p.26

articles.[11] He had completely changed his views about orthodox Benthamite economics and writing his articles anonymously suited him then. He was able to give vent to his feelings on subjects that before he had had to refrain from so doing, as they would not have been approved by the Benthamite Association.

That sense of uncertainty that Mill experienced was a forerunner of his coming break with Benthamism. From his earliest memories, he was trained for that purpose as an end result. He was subconsciously aware of the disappointment that his leaving the movement would cause his father. But it was something that passing through the crisis had stamped indelibly on his mind, there was no turning back, especially now that both himself and Harriet had found a mutual interest. Both had written essays on the *Subjection of Women* and laid them aside for future development. Equality of the sexes was becoming one of the dominant features in that era. It was an ideal opportunity for both to combine their knowledge on that subject, which was also freely discussed among the group. It gradually gained precedence over other social articles.[12]

But it was not until thirty-seven years later that John Mill decided to bring the *Subjection of Women* up to publishing standard. John and Harriet were two people whose ideas for the most part blended, but who still upheld their differences of opinions. Harriet was far more radical in her ideas than Mill, whose logical mind always persuaded him to be cautious. On the subject of education, for instance, Mill held that a woman's first concern should continue to be her home and family. Higher education would enable her to share more intelligently in her husband's occupation and other interests. She would also become a better hostess. Harriet's ideas were more objective, she felt that educated women should enter any occupational field that they wanted to, and share the household responsibilities. That question, of the wife contributing to the family income, continued to puzzle Mill.[13]

---

[11] Ibid., John & Harriet Mill, p.27
[12] Ibid., John & Harriet Mill, p.21
[13] Ibid., John & Harriet Mill, p.23

Analysis of John Stuart Mill's Life

Europeans, in that period, suffered a lot from ill-health brought on by climatic and other conditions for which no cure had yet been found. Both John and Harriet had suffered from tuberculosis, and on several occasions both had to spend long periods in tropical countries. They had decided to try out a six-month period of separation, which raised the hopes of John Taylor that Harriet would break with John Mill. But it did not work as far as their attachment to each other was concerned. All parties concerned maintained high principles, and Harriet returned to her family. A lot of changes took place during those years of ill-health and uncertainty. Mill retired from the Radical group when the members became disillusioned by parliamentary defeat of their theories. It was believed by some that his relationship with Harriet was the cause, but Mill would hardly have abandoned a cause that he believed in because of gossip.

The sudden collapse of Radicalism did make Mill reconsider many aspects of the overall conditions that led up to it. The main contention of the Philosophical Radicals dealt with the ruling elite and the power that they had over the lower classes. That was the main topic. They also saw the Church, universities and legal systems as allied to the aristocracy. That incensed Radicals such as Jeremy Bentham and James Mill. When it became apparent that Radicalism had lost its battle, the members shifted to other intellectual activities, and soon forgot about the Movement which they had found to have many flaws. John Mill left politics and started to write on historical topics. In many ways, the crisis that he passed through helped to clarify his thoughts. He was better able to cope with any disappointment over the collapse of the Radicals and concentrated on more scholarly work. He published *A System of Logic* in 1843 and the *Principles of Political Economy* in 1848.[14]

As usual, the question of Harriet's personality and general qualifications aroused the interest of Mill's friends. Thomas Carlyle described her as "an interesting and romantic figure with a high

---

[14] Ibid., John & Harriet Mill, p.31

degree of insight and purpose."[15] That was high praise from such an eminent author. In his autobiography, John Mill left no doubt about his estimation of her when he said:

> ". . . more of a poet than Carlyle, more of a thinker than himself, like Shelley in temperament and organization but his superior in thought and intellect . . ."[16]

John Mill's friend and first biographer, Alexander Bain, tried to prevent the publication of such excessive praise when he read it in 1873. He wrote to that effect to Mill's step-daughter, Helen Taylor, but his objections were overruled, and Mill's views were retained. In his published works, William Fox also paid her high tribute when he wrote telling his daughter of her death, saying:

> "Mrs. Mill died on the 3rd at Avignon. She would not have objected to being buried there, in the ground in which Petrarch has given a wide-world fame: and of which it might . . . be said, 'A greater than Laura is here'."[17]

It was discovered that Laura and Harriet had a lot in common. They were both married with children before they found true love, and both came to rest at Avignon in the end. By contrast to the above-mentioned praise of Harriet's excellent qualities, there were numerous negative assessments made of her by people with whom she associated in the Radical group. The most unkind characterization of her was made by Diana Trilling who remarked that, she had "nothing more than a vestpocket flashlight of a mind" and went on to describe her as "one of the meanest and dullest ladies in literary history."[18] It was further argued that the

---

[15] Ibid., John & Harriet Mill, p.31
[16] Ibid., John & Harriet Mill, p.32
[17] Ibid., John & Harriet Mill, p.33
[18] Ibid., John & Harriet Mill, p.35

emphasis credited to her for moulding John Mill's life was grossly exaggerated. A mind as highly developed as his would not easily adopt ideas that were not principally sound, regardless of whose mind they originated from.

Political attitudes have a lot of bearing on the kind of assessment made of members of a group. It is interesting to note that those who spoke negatively of Harriet came from the Philosophic Radicals, or scholars interested in the circle, and those who gave a positive assessment came from the Unitarian Radicals. There were significant differences between the two groups in theory, politics and morality. The Philosophic Radicals represented moral righteousness and theoretical commitment to both parliamentary Reform and Utilitarianism. The Unitarian Radicals were unconventional and artistic. They were also committed to a wide range of political and social domestic affairs.

Mill's peers dismissed the assessments made as exaggerated and lacking in understanding, especially where Mill was concerned. The hypothesis that anyone, much less a woman, could hold such sway over his mind was not acceptable. While all that debate absorbed public attention, nothing was done to obtain direct historical evidence. Access to the Mill-Taylor correspondence could easily have been obtained at that time, a privilege that was not granted to earlier writers. It has always been claimed that no clear picture of the true relationship between John and Harriet has been brought to light. Most of what has been said about them was based on assumption. That they were compatible and had ideas in common was evident by their joint publications from 1840 on. Mill made a statement of their joint work in his *Political Economy*.[19] Those manuscripts are now a part of the Mill-Taylor Collection in the British Library of Political and Economic Science (London School of Economics), and were first published by Hayek in 1951.[19]

There was some speculation as to why, if Harriet was as good as she was made out to be, did Mill have everything published under his name alone. Evidence was given that Harriet was not completely

---

[19] Ibid., John & Harriet Mill, p.22

satisfied with that arrangement and consulted her husband on the matter. He was against any action that would draw attention to her and revive criticism that had quietened down. He told her it would be in bad taste to have her name mentioned in any dedication. Harriet was naturally disappointed that social conventions had forced her to remain unacknowledged by the reading public.[20]

Recent scholars who have delved deeply into John Mill's life, trying to get another glimpse of his elusive personality, revealed that he was not the hard scientific "logic machine" that his image presented to the world. Basil Willey (an English scholar) saw him rather in the light of a Renaissance man, with well-developed faculties, striving to attain the utmost of man's ability intellectually.[21] When one reflects on his simplicity of manner, even to the point of being naive at times, that description comes nearer to being the true one of him. Max Lerner also pointed out that, for all his show of rationalism, Mill was a "committed and incurable romantic" who saw everything in more than life-size proportions, and wrote:

> "Here was no ... sawdust-stuffed Victorian moralist, no prim and unctuous spokesman for a carefully ordered world. Here was rather a man of strong passions, large vision, tenacious will, powerful intellect, who used and fused all his qualities in the service of a vision of a better world for all his fellow men."[22]

As soon as John and Harriet were married, they started to practise the principles that they advocated. Perfect equality between the sexes. A clear call for that state to be put into force was the theme of John's and Harriet's famous essays *On Liberty*, and that sentiment was again echoed in Harriet's essay on *Enfranchisement of Women*.

---

[20] Ibid., John & Harriet Mill, p.41
[21] Ibid., John & Harriet Mill, p.43
[22] Ibid., John & Harriet Mill, p.44

"We deny the right of any portion of the species to decide for another portion . . . what is and what is not their 'proper sphere'. The proper sphere for all human beings is the largest and highest which they are able to attain to. What this is, cannot be ascertained, without complete liberty of choice."[23]

Harriet's son, Algernon Taylor, enlightened the public a bit more about John Mill's musical talent. He was fond of performing on the piano, but only when asked. He composed as he played on the spur of the moment. His music was "rich in feeling, vigour and suggestiveness." From 1853 until Harriet's death in 1858, there were numerous separations as they each in turn sought Southern weather. Stillinger saw their married years more as a period of correspondence than of companionship.[24] That was especially noticeable when Mill's doctor ordered him out of England from December 1854 to the end of the summer of 1855. There were also other months spent in Italy, Sicily and Greece. Mill was conscious that time was running out. There was always the undercurrent urgency to complete their unfinished work before death claimed them.

On one occasion he wrote:

"We must finish the best we have got to say, and not only that, but publish it while we are alive. I do not see what living depository there is likely to be of our thoughts, or who in this weak generation that is growing up will even be capable of thoroughly mastering and assimilating your ideas, much less of re-originating them - so we must write them and print them, and then they can wait until there are again thinkers."[25]

---

[23] Ibid., John & Harriet Mill, p.46
[24] Ibid., John & Harriet Mill, p.47
[25] Ibid., John & Harriet Mill, p.48

That passage gave every indication of how relentlessly they must have driven themselves even when feeling ill and not inclined to work. Although Mill would appear to be presumptuous in his summing up of the I.Q. of the following generation, he must be given credit for not being able to tolerate indifference in educational matters on account of his unusual background. Had they both not finished the work that they had started, the manuscripts would either have disappeared or been added to by someone else who would have changed the theme of most.

If there remained any lingering doubts that John and Harriet Mill could not maintain a friendship without impropriety, her reply to his letter of urgency clarified the situation when she described the general masses:

> "... those poor wretches who cannot conceive friendship but in sex - nor believe that expediency and the consideration for feelings of others can conquer sensuality..."[26]

Although the Mills had very advanced ideas about the status of women, marriage and divorce laws, education and basic human rights, they were very much Victorian and conservative about relationships. But that was not the issue that motivated their efforts to bring about changes in the law. It was a wide variety of falsely upheld notions that placed women in a category that gave them no scope to improve their condition, nor were they able to move away from the narrow confines in which they were placed. John and Harriet fought for liberation from that kind of bondage. Mill tried to emphasize the seriousness of that issue in his *A System of Logic* where he expressed the belief that for best results:

> "... social planning and political action should rely primarily on scientific knowledge, not on authority, custom, revelation, or prescription..."[27]

---

[26] Ibid., John & Harriet Mill, p.49
[27] Ibid., *Encyclopaedia of Philosophy*, p.315

A System of Logic was considered to be superior to any book existing in that field because of its clear version of social and religious problems as they existed then. Mill was convinced that experience in philosophy was the best way to encourage development of society along liberal lines.

In his last book of the *Logic, The Moral Sciences,* Mill searched for clues to determine the natural laws of human behaviour. He searched through various modes of inquiry in the different physical sciences to find which most suited his investigations. He even sketched an advanced outline of what a completed science of man would be in the future.[28] In an estimation of how far social science had progressed, he felt that the basic laws of psychology were well established, but the science of "ethology", which he had hoped to found himself, eluded him. He gave up working on it shortly after he published *A System of Logic.* Mill was not discouraged. The Comte philosophy had shown that opinion always passes through the same three phases. Men try to understand the universe in theological terms, metaphysical terms, and scientific terms.[29] Mill looked forward to the time when no important branch of human affairs would be left to unscientific surmise.

Mill believed that we all must know some things intuitively, but whatever can be known only by intuition is beyond the realm of rational discussion or experimental test. Intuitive knowledge can be mistaken for dogmatic opinion, and he endeavoured to limit the use of intuitive instinct. In his *Logic,* he argued that it was not a necessary ingredient for mathematics, logic or natural science. To be able to distinguish what is directly given to consciousness from what is already there, it is necessary to investigate the origins of the present contents of the mind which, to a large extent, is impossible as the minds of infants are not accessible to us. It would entail the study of a whole generation for modes on mental behaviour, and that would only produce facts that were not original.

Writing on ethics, Mill again attacked "Intuitionism", which he

---

[28] Ibid., *Encyclopaedia of Philosophy,* p.317
[29] Ibid., *Encyclopaedia of Philosophy,* p.318

claimed in his *Autobiography*, "is the great intellectual support of false doctrines and bad institutions because it enabled established opinions and intense feeling to dispense with the necessity of justifying itself by reason." He also held that it was specially devised for consecrating deep-seated prejudices. Mill had dealt with Intuitionism all his life as it was closely connected to Utilitarianism. That was why he elaborated so extensively on its qualities in his *A System of Logic*. That knowledge enabled him to promote moral directives other than the Utilitarian principle. But Utilitarianism was valuable in providing a rational basis for the criticism of secondary rules, such as the development of individual character upon which Mill placed so much emphasis.[30]

Mill saw in his own times the widespread breakdown of Christian moral belief, he realized the importance of ethical methods to form a unified society. Although he was a disciple of Utilitarian ethics, he believed that an action was only right if it demonstrated a larger balance of good in any given circumstance. John Mill modified the views of both James Mill and Jeremy Bentham on that subject. They were projecting a narrow view that did not rely on Social progress, but purely on impersonal arrangements that compelled participants to leave human personality out of account. John Mill tried to make the Benthamite philosophy more acceptable and, although his ethical writings (especially those on Utilitarianism) have been criticized, it was acknowledged that they contained influential philosophical information on liberal humanistic morality.[31]

Throughout his discourse on Logic, Mill placed directives that did not include Utilitarian principles in a prominent position. He saw that principle to be so abstract, that the chances of it being actually applied were slim. The only exception would be in cases where secondary rules clashed with each other. Mill derived satisfaction as it served as a valuable source for criticism.[32] It also

---

[30] Ibid., *Encyclopaedia of Philosophy*, p.320
[31] Ibid., *Encyclopaedia of Philosophy*, p.319
[32] Ibid., *Encyclopaedia of Philosophy*, p.320

made him do in-depth studies on other disciplines. For instance, the theory of "free will" made him conscious of the importance of self-development and the power behind the desire to find adequate ways of doing so. Under the influence of that drive, he contemplated the time when individuals would become responsible for their own characters.

John Mill's Utilitarianism came under attack far more frequently than any of the others. He tried to bring the different kinds of intellectual pleasures into a clearer focus, with the intention of summing up their qualities and making a selection. Instead, he became involved in a controversy that carried overtones of human rights. He also felt that it was up to him to support the Utilitarian principle, and was accused by G. E. Moore of committing the "naturalistic fallacy".[33]

John Mill never accepted anything at face value. He examined each issue, then decided on the good and bad points before arriving at a conclusion. The Democratic government was no exception. He was convinced that citizens who lived under such a regime had to be well educated, and be tolerant of opposing views, for it to be a success. They must be prepared to sacrifice some of their immediate interests to make it workable for the good of society. But Mill was more concerned about the tendency of democracies to overlook individuals and minority groups and their special needs. The theme of his writings on social and political philosophy centred on those issues and how to devise better ways to improve conditions.

Looking at Socialism from an objective point of view, Mill had to reconsider some of his strongly held convictions on "Individualism", a fact that he had thrust to the back of his mind, but it could no longer be ignored. In all his years as an economist, he had entertained doubts on the theory of blending socialism and economic ideas. He feared that Socialism, as a comprehensive discipline, would lend strength to the suppression of individuality. Later on, in his *On Liberty*, he argued that:

---

[33] Ibid., *Encyclopaedia of Philosophy*, p.320

> "the sole end for which mankind are warranted, individually or collectively, in interfering with the liberty of action of any of their number, is self-protection..."[34]

That continued to be his main contention throughout the book which he believed, of all his works, to be of the most enduring value, especially in the areas of "freedom of thought and discussion". It is essential to clarify an opinion before declaring it valid. The quality that made *On Liberty* enduring was the complete unison of ideas between John and Harriet when they were writing it. As he pointed out:

> "When two persons have their thoughts and speculations completely in common: when all subjects of intellectual or moral interest are discussed between them in daily life, and probed to much greater depths than are usually or conveniently sounded in writings intended for general readers: when they set out from the same principles, and arrive at their conclusions by processes pursued jointly, it is of little consequence in respect to the question of originality, which of them holds the pen..."[35]

Looking back on all their years of friendship before and after marriage, Mill felt that all his published works carried elements of Harriet's thinking and he did not hesitate to give her credit when she introduced new ideas. He was well aware that he excelled in the scientific field, logic, metaphysics, political economy and politics, and was not willing to learn from everybody. Consequently, he erred in other disciplines that he had not imbibed as thoroughly as the sciences. Working closely with Harriet, he was able to correct those errors that were more or less minor ones, and adjust his thoughts on a practical level of exchanging ideas with others. He discovered that Carlyle and other thinkers (especially German)

---

[34] Ibid., *Encyclopaedia of Philosophy*, p.320
[35] Ibid., *Autobiography of John Stuart Mill*, p.171

were strongly opposed to the mode of thought he expressed that was veiled in mystical phraseology. Mill changed his views.[36]

Mill paid tribute to A. Bain for his assistance in helping him to prepare *A System of Logic*. After going carefully through the manuscript before it was sent to the press, Bain passed on a number of examples and illustrations on science that enriched the work.[37] But of all the books written, *On Liberty* was the one that he associated most with Harriet. They had worked very closely on it, both intellectually and introspectively. Through her influence, he had overcome the tendency to resist other opinions passed on. On the contrary, he later became anxious to learn from all who generated new ideas. Through her just measure given to different considerations, Harriet proved to be of eminent value to Mill's mental development along those lines. He realized that he could quite easily have become overly concerned with governmental affairs, which could have persuaded him to be either an extreme radical or a democrat and so robbed him of his free will.

John Mill's active mind became very confused with all those new transitions of ideas, and the uprooting of beliefs considered to be permanent. Mentally wading through several alternative suggestions as to whether he should retain some former ideas, he found that certain doctrines persisted in holding their own and that caused him to exercise willpower, along with his knowledge on the subject of what should be discarded and what had fundamental values. Although Mill rejected Utilitarianism eventually, he still regarded certain aspects of that discipline as a sound basis for all schools of philosophy. His break from it was more with his father's and Bentham's version.

Mill defended the Movement on the grounds of misrepresentation of its true meaning. The utility creed, that advocated "happiness" as the greatest principle, implied much more than the light frivolous fun that the word conjured up. The Utilitarian form of happiness concerned mental power and how it

---

[36] Ibid., *Autobiography of John Stuart Mill*, p.177
[37] Ibid., *Autobiography of John Stuart Mill*, p.174

was distributed in any given society. James Mill and Jeremy Bentham practised a very narrow and biased kind that gave it a bad start for those who did not read beneath the surface of its literature. Its purpose, as a theory of morality, was meant to set guide-lines for all social and governmental societies which, if governed correctly and satisfied the public needs as far as it was possible to do so, would generate a feeling of happiness in the minds of all those who perpetuated the custom.

It had been taken for granted that most of those who were equally acquainted with both versions of "happiness" showed a marked preference for the one representing their higher faculties. Not many human creatures would deliberately cultivate the habits of lower animals, nor would they want to be classified as such. Against those two doctrines, another school of thought appeared on the scene and denied the claim that happiness could in any way affect human life or actions. They claimed that mankind could do without it, that all noble human beings only attained that standard by learning the lesson of renunciation.[38]

On account of its rigid rules, Utilitarianism was considered as lacking sympathy in its teachings, and had the effect of lessening moral feelings toward individuals. They were also accused of being influenced in their method of assessment of the qualities of the persons concerned and that was not considered to be ethical.[39] Claiming that the proof of a good character was shown by good actions, and refusing to accept other mental attitudes, made Utilitarianism unpopular with some sections of society. But, as John Mill pointed out, Utilitarianism did not introduce "difference of opinion" as moral questioning into the world, it only attempted to find a tangible and intelligible method of coping with such issues.[40]

Where Utilitarians failed in making their creed popular was in

---

[38] John Stuart Mill, *Utilitarianism*. Oskar Piest, editor (The Bobbs-Merrill Company, Inc., 1957), pp.16-17
[39] Ibid., Mill, *Utilitarianism*, pp.25,26
[40] Ibid., pp.26,27

not having enough artistic perception. They were much too forthright in their approach and gave the impression of having dogmatic tendencies. John Mill, who could not have been accused of negligence in his research or criticism of any work that he had undertaken, especially on the subject of Utilitarianism that he had been trained for from childhood, found no significant differences in the basic operations of that doctrine to any other such organisation. It displayed the normal amount of rigorous discipline and laxity that was standard procedure. He discovered that misunderstanding of its ethical doctrines, and prejudice against some opinions, helped to create a sense of suspicion about the movement.[41]

Utilitarianism started on its journey with a false precept that appeared to have followed it through its career. Some were undoubtedly not what the public wanted, but there were others that worked equally well. Mill's ability to imbibe and maintain a variety of disciplines also enabled him to retain portions of the Utilitarian doctrine that he felt were consistent with good socialism, and he defended its principles when they were unnecessarily attacked. Working on the premise that some good can be derived from all groups that attract the public, any opinion given by him whether in condemnation or praise, would be just. *Encyclopaedia Americana* had this to say of John Mill:

> "The distinctive feature of Mill's A System of Logic (1843), was the proposition that the rules of reasoning are obtained from experience, as opposed to the traditional view that they are a part of the mind's construction or of the universe..."[42]

Mill's assertion that logic is the method of testing factual validity of statements, made him the forerunner of scientific methods. He

---

[41] Ibid., pp.27,28
[42] *Encyclopaedia Americana*, International edition (Grolier Incorporated (Int. Headquarters) Connecticut, 1981), Vol.19, p.119

also believed that mankind is more prone to do good initially.

At the age of twelve, John Mill began to write a serious history of the Roman Government. It is not surprising that he described himself as a "dry, hard logical machine" on attaining manhood. At that age, he had already read Gibbon, Robertsin and Hume, among other historians, as well as all the Greek authors. In his thirteenth year, he had mastered algebra and geometry. He began a serious study in logic and classical literature, and in 1819, he did a complete course in political economy.[43] Later, he was persuaded to stand for Westminster, and became involved with parliamentary duties for a time. But he found that these did not absorb his attention as much as he thought they would. He was not sorry when he lost his seat and was able to return to his literary career. He was also busy writing the fourth volume of his *Dissertation*, which was published in 1869. Mill got a lot of help from his step-daughter, Helen Taylor, on that fourth volume, he spoke very highly of her. He alluded to her as "another prize in the lottery of life" after the death of his wife. Helen took care of him until his death at Avignon in 1873. Three days before he died, he had walked fifteen miles on a botanical excursion.[44]

Mill saw religion more in terms of a social vehicle, whose usefulness could be attributed to the influence it instilled in moral code that served as a guide to public opinion. He believed that the effect of religion on individuals sprang from the need of human beings to have an incentive to move them to action and direct their emotions to an ideal object. He visualized a religion of humanity that would surpass the supernatural and develop unselfish feelings. It would also mean freedom from intellectual wilful blunders that have in many instances proved to be a hindrance. Rather, it would encourage the willingness to find ways to remove the evil connected with most religious institutions.

Mill brought to every discipline that he studied fresh ideas that

---

[43] *Dictionary of National Biography*, Sidney Lee, editor (Smith, Elder & Company, London, 1894) Vol.37, pp.391,396,397
[44] Ibid., *Dictionary of National Biography*, pp.396,397

were feasible and accepted by most of those who read his works. *The New Encyclopaedia Britannica* described him as a man of extreme simplicity, whose influence on contemporary thought can scarcely be overestimated. His name continues to come up in philosophical discussions. He left behind a body of doctrine and technical terms on subjects that proved to be useful in the classroom. Because of his sound logical reasoning, he came to be regarded as a personification of certain tendencies in philosophy necessary to all who think deeply on the subject.[45]

John Mill revealed himself to be capable of solving practically all the difficult situations that people encountered in their daily lives with the utmost intelligence. Few, if any, have since searched so diligently for the purpose behind the actions of mankind. No situation, however insignificant it might appear to others, was too trivial for his attention, and where possible, he improved the existing condition or suggested other methods.

---

[45] *The New Encyclopaedia Britannica* (Chicago, 1985) Vol.24, p.103